T0388266

365 Quotes for School Leaders

Start your morning with a daily dose of inspiration! Bestselling author Danny Steele, known for his motivational @steelethoughts tweets, brings you a powerful quote for every day of the year.

You'll find quotes on topics such as school culture, supporting your staff, effective leadership, positive communication, and more.

Read them to kick off your morning, to wind down at night, or whenever you need to recharge. Share them at staff meetings and workshops to set the tone or spark conversation. The uplifting, insightful quotes will remind you of the positive impact you're having on your school, each and every day.

Danny Steele (@steelethoughts) is a principal from Birmingham, Alabama, and has worked in public education for over 28 years. In 2016, he was named Alabama's Secondary Principal of the Year. He has presented at numerous state and national conferences and writes an educational leadership blog that has received over 5 million page views.

Also Available from Routledge Eye On Education
(www.routledge.com/k-12)

**365 Quotes for Teachers:
Inspiration and Motivation for Every Day of the Year**
Danny Steele

Essential Truths for Principals
Danny Steele and Todd Whitaker

Essential Truths for Teachers
Danny Steele and Todd Whitaker

Education Write Now, Volume I
Edited by Jeffrey Zoul and Joe Mazza

**Education Write Now, Volume II: Top Strategies for
Improving Relationships and Culture**
Edited by Jeffrey Zoul and Sanée Bell

**Education Write Now, Volune III: Solutions to
Common Challenges n Your School or Classroom**
Edited by Jeffrey Zoul and Sanée Bell

365 Quotes for School Leaders

Inspiration and Motivation for Every Day of the Year

Danny Steele

NEW YORK AND LONDON

First published 2022
by Routledge
605 Third Avenue, New York, NY 10158

and by Routledge
2 Park Square, Milton Park, Abingdon, Oxon, OX14 4RN

Routledge is an imprint of the Taylor & Francis Group, an informa business

© 2022 Taylor & Francis

The right of Danny Steele to be identified as author of this work has
been asserted by him in accordance with sections 77 and 78 of the
Copyright, Designs and Patents Act 1988.

All rights reserved. No part of this book may be reprinted or
reproduced or utilised in any form or by any electronic, mechanical,
or other means, now known or hereafter invented, including
photocopying and recording, or in any information storage or
retrieval system, without permission in writing from the publishers.

Trademark notice: Product or corporate names may be trademarks
or registered trademarks, and are used only for identification and
explanation without intent to infringe.

Library of Congress Cataloging-in-Publication Data
A catalog record for this book has been requested

ISBN: 978-1-032-10765-3 (hbk)
ISBN: 978-1-032-07628-7 (pbk)
ISBN: 978-1-003-21693-3 (ebk)

DOI: 10.4324/9781003216933

Typeset in Palatino
by Apex CoVantage, LLC

Contents

Acknowledgements vi

Meet the Author vii

Introduction 1

365 Quotes 3

Index of Quotes by Topic 186

Acknowledgements

With every project, there are important individuals to acknowledge. This book would not have happened if my brother, David, hadn't encouraged me to begin networking with other educators. Engaging with other professionals on social media has transformed my career. I could not ask for a more supportive editor. I'm grateful to Lauren Davis and her team at Routledge for believing in my message and supporting this project. I'm grateful to all the educators out there with whom I have connected on social media. There are too many of you to mention, but thank you for engaging. Thank you for supporting me, and thank you for sharing my thoughts over the years. And to my wife, Holley . . . thank you for being so patient with me as I navigated the "Twitterverse." You have my gratitude; you have my respect; and you have my heart.

Meet the Author

Dr. Danny Steele is a principal from Birmingham, Alabama, and has worked in public education for over 28 years. In addition to serving as a principal at multiple levels, he has worked as a teacher, coach, assistant principal, and university instructor. In 2005, Danny was recognized as the Secondary Assistant Principal of the Year for the state of Alabama, and in 2016, he was named Alabama's Secondary Principal of the Year. He has presented at numerous state and national conferences, and he writes an educational leadership blog that has received over 5 million page views. Danny has an undergraduate degree in History from Covenant College (Lookout Mountain, Georgia); he has a graduate degree in History from the University of Alabama, Birmingham; he has an Educational Specialist degree in Educational Administration and an Educational Doctorate degree in Educational Leadership—both from Samford University (Birmingham, Alabama). He lives with his wife, Holley, in Birmingham, Alabama. They have three children; DJ, Will, and Elizabeth.

Introduction

I first started sharing my educational thoughts on Twitter about five years ago. I quickly realized there are thousands of educators out there who appreciate being validated in their own beliefs about education. They appreciate being reminded of their purpose. And so my journey began . . . tweeting about the core values that drive school leaders. The quotes in this book are drawn from that journey. Quotes can serve as guideposts as you navigate the challenges in your career. They can crystalize your thoughts; they can underscore your values; and they can clarify your priorities. It is my hope that you will see yourselves in these pages—that you will be reconnected to the heart of leadership and that you will feel supported and encouraged to continue in your noble profession. These quotes are meant to motivate you, to challenge you, and to help you keep your job in perspective. I hope you enjoy them. I hope they inspire you to push on as you work to care about students, support teachers, and lead the type of school where kids enjoy learning and adults enjoy working.

365 Quotes

1

~~~~~~

The first day of school shouldn't be about the syllabus, the rules, or even a lesson. It should be about the students! It should be about ensuring they understand this class is a safe place, a positive place, and a place that gives them hope for a great school year.

2

Administrators . . . one of the best things you can ever do for teachers is to treat them like professionals.

3

An organization where the staff cannot ever question or challenge the boss is not a healthy organization. Leaders . . . if you create a culture in which staff never feel free to disagree with you to your face, be assured they are doing it behind your back.

4

Teachers want to work in a school where:

- they are supported when dealing with students and parents.
- their professional judgment is respected.
- they have a voice in school-wide decisions.
- they feel their work is noticed and appreciated.

5

It's not enough to teach kids. The best schools help their kids feel valued and connected.

6

School culture is like the wind. It can be hard to explain . . . but everyone feels it.

7

Teachers don't always need a new strategy, a new activity, or a new resource. Sometimes . . . what they need is some encouragement. They need to be reminded that they're professionals, that they are good at what they do, and that what they are doing every day really does matter.

8

You don't change culture through emails and memos. You change it through relationships . . . one conversation at a time.

9

Good school culture doesn't happen by accident. You build it every day with what you value and with how you spend your time.

10

In many ways, you hope to be predictable as a leader. If the staff know what you value, they will know what drives your decisions. If they don't know your values, you're not leading from the heart. And you're not leading effectively.

11

I think it's a mistake for leaders to be preoccupied with supervision. That sort of focus implies that your staff are employees to be managed rather than professionals who want to be led.

12

I know we're supposed to make our decisions based on the needs of the students . . . but we can never discount the needs of the adults in the school. They're the ones taking care of the kids. And they want what's best for students as well.

13

I think the first step in effective leadership is being a good colleague to those you wish to lead.

14

Sometimes teachers don't need their administrators to inspire them, motivate them, or even lead them. Sometimes what teachers need . . . is for their administrators to listen to them, understand them, and validate their experiences.

15

Leaders can bring positive energy into the school. They can provide meaningful support for and genuinely communicate how much they value their staff. It doesn't have to take extra money or extraordinary expertise. But it does require passion for the work.

16

Some thoughts on raising staff morale:

- Trust staff to do their job . . . and give them the freedom to do it. Respect their professionalism.
- Thank staff for doing their job; never take it for granted.
- Listen to staff's concerns and act on them when you can.

17

Leaders need to be willing to listen to bad news. They need to be willing to hear uncomfortable truths. And they need to create a culture in the organization where everyone feels OK speaking up.

18

Leadership isn't about telling people where to go; it's about helping people on the journey.

19

If we want people to take pride in their work, we need to show them we value their work. If we want people to take initiative, we need to show them we value their contribution. Awesomeness doesn't typically happen in a vacuum; it happens in the right culture.

20

If leaders are making all the decisions by themselves, they're not really leading; they're dictating.

21

Every time a leader collaborates, he or she communicates to colleagues that they are valued. Every time a leader collaborates, he or she also learns information that will allow for a more effective decision. The collaboration also ensures stronger support for the decision.

22

We will come back here and do it again tomorrow. Sometimes . . . we don't feel like coming to work. Sometimes . . . it is a grind. Teaching and leading can be hard . . . and emotionally draining. But we will come back tomorrow. That's what we do . . . because our students need us; our staff need us.

23

Every time you communicate, you run the risk of being misunderstood. That reality shouldn't discourage you from communicating; it should underscore the value of continued conversation.

24

When you talk about the importance of teachers supporting and encouraging their students, remember that's exactly what you should be doing for your teachers.

25

I think managers are working to hold their people accountable for their job. I think leaders are trying to create the conditions where their people hold themselves accountable for their job. The former is a culture of compliance. The latter, a culture of excellence.

26

Leaders don't always have the answers . . . but they can always demonstrate compassion. They probably can't fix every problem . . . but they can always show support. They might not have the expertise . . . but they can always collaborate with those who do.

27

Principals like for teachers to provide engaging instruction. Well, teachers and students like for their principal to provide engaging leadership. It means walking around, having lots of conversations, being a cheerleader, working collaboratively, and caring about everyone in the school.

28

When schools don't create positive experiences for students . . . they fail at their most basic mission. We must create positive experiences for kids if we want them to have a good attitude toward learning. Good experiences for EVERY student!

29

Managers care about compliance. Leaders care about culture. (When the culture is right, "compliance" is a moot point . . . because employees are driven to excel.)

30

Managers stop by to make sure you're working. Leaders stop by to encourage you in your work.

31

It's good for teachers to realize that their students have some heavy stuff with which they're dealing at home . . . and it's good for administrators to realize that their teachers have some heavy stuff with which they're dealing at home too.

32

Good leaders don't have all the answers . . . and they're not threatened by all the questions.

33

Being an instructional leader doesn't always mean you are providing expertise in teaching and learning. Sometimes . . . it just means you are helping to shape the conditions in which your teachers can thrive. Sometimes it's just about building the right culture.

34

I know we're in a "kid business" . . . but it's hard to be an effective administrator if you don't love teachers too. They do the core work of the school, and it's crucial that they feel valued and supported.

35

The people who work with you day in and day out . . . they know the real you. Ultimately, it's not about what we put out there on social media; it's about how we treat the people right in front of us. It's not about talking a good game; it's about playing a good game.

36

I don't know all the rules for being successful . . . but I know the first one: you need to enjoy what you're doing.

37

When employees are underperforming, maybe it's not about them being "slackers." Maybe it's not about them lacking pride. MAYBE . . . it's about them lacking confidence. Maybe . . . it's about them not feeling competent. Good leaders are sensitive to this and work to empower their people.

38

Good leaders are sensitive to staff morale. They can't solve every problem . . . but they can always support their staff, and they can always care about them. In my experience, those two things go a long way.

39

The educators who are constantly sharing messages of "positivity" are not in denial about the very real challenges that educators face. They just realize that a good attitude gives them the best chance of solving those problems, and they understand that a negative outlook destroys motivation.

40

Teachers appreciate candor, transparency, and vulnerability from their leaders. And they don't ever take that stuff for granted.

41

Maslow's "hierarchy of needs" does not just apply to students; it applies to teachers as well. They are in the pyramid too. Administrators are more effective when they are mindful of that reality.

42

Here's a tip for young administrators: Give teachers the benefit of the doubt. You will never lead them effectively if you don't learn to trust them.

43

It's hard for teachers to fill the buckets of their students when their own buckets are runnin' low. That's why good administrators are always looking to support, encourage, reinforce, and inspire their teachers.

44

Three ways to build rapport with teachers:

- Spend some time appreciating their instruction . . . not just critiquing it.
- Spend some time asking them about their family.
- Spend some time laughing and goofing off with them.

(Note: To build rapport . . . you have to spend some time.)

45

No administrator ever built culture sitting in their office. No administrator ever improved their school by doing paperwork. I know there is administrivia to be done, but as school leaders . . . you need to figure out how to make your time count.

46

You don't build rapport with teachers through emails. You do it by walking the halls and being in their rooms. You build it through conversations.

47

Good principals are committed to these three things:

- supporting teachers.
- connecting with kids.
- building positive culture.

48

Leaders have flaws. They are all human. But good leaders champion a cause that is greater than them. Our cause is children . . . and creating for them a brighter future. And that is greater than all of us.

49

You want teachers to be sensitive to the home life of kids. Well . . . you need to be sensitive to the home life of their teachers. They deal with divorce, depression, family illness, and other stresses that can have a profound impact. They need compassion too.

50

What are the conditions in your classroom and school that contribute to the likelihood that students will make good decisions . . . or bad decisions? Ultimately . . . your actions, your attitude, and the environment you create are the only things you can control.

51

When teachers do excellent work, administrators should complement them. When students do excellent work, teachers should complement them. We shouldn't go home with complements left unsaid. We all need encouragement.

52

It's a mistake for administrators to assume all their teachers are confident in what they're doing. Some need more encouragement and support than others . . . just like students.

53

One of the first steps in becoming a great leader is recognizing that your own attitude affects the attitude of those you wish to lead.

54

It's important for all administrators to recognize that, first and foremost, teachers are not looking for "instructional leadership" . . . they are looking for support. And when they feel the support, they are much more receptive to the instructional leadership.

55

It's true that administrators should "inspect what they expect." Accountability is a real thing. But they should always assume teachers are trying to do the right thing. Every teacher wants to be a good teacher, and this assumption provides a good foundation for the teacher–administrator relationship.

56

As administrators, we don't usually get to have the same "light bulb moments" that teachers have with kids in their class. Our rewarding moments are when we can support teachers . . . when we can do something to lighten their load and make their tough job a little easier.

57

It doesn't take much to make a teacher's day. Let them wear jeans, bring them chocolate, or serve them homemade soup. It doesn't take much . . . but you have to know your teachers; you have to know what THEY appreciate. And "teacher appreciation" must be a priority more than one week out of the year.

58

Principals don't set the tone at the faculty meeting. They set the tone in the hallway, in the classrooms . . . and with all the little conversations.

59

Encouraging words never get old. Ever. If you want to make a difference for someone . . . build them up with your words. They don't have to be special words . . . or profound words. They just have to be from the heart.

60

Staff members might respect the position and respect the title . . . but loyalty is inspired and earned by the leader.

61

To me . . . there is never a time when staff morale is irrelevant. It's great when you talk to teachers enough to know not just what they're thinking . . . but how they're feeling. And then really care about it.

62

~~~~~~

It's great for administrators to pop in classes. But maybe they should withhold judgment if they happen to see something that they don't like. It's only a snapshot, and they may have missed some brilliance five minutes earlier.

63

~~~~~~

Leaders . . . if the adults around you don't feel supported by you . . . they don't care about your vision, your expertise, or your brilliant ideas. They just don't.

64

If you're a leader, I think one of your main jobs is to celebrate the successes of those around you. It validates institutional values. It creates organizational momentum. It elevates staff morale. It generates professional pride. And it creates a climate where people can thrive.

65

If you're trying to build the right culture, ask yourself this question: "Do my staff feel valued?" I think everything else flows from that. When the adults feel valued, they work harder; they're upbeat; and they have more emotional energy to invest in their students.

66

I love students . . . and I always will. But the most important lesson I learned as an administrator was that my primary job was to support the staff. (And this support allows teachers to care about the kids more effectively.)

67

Instructional leaders are not effective because of their curriculum expertise; they are effective because of their ability to support, challenge, and motivate teachers.

68

I don't think it's possible for administrators to spend too much time learning about the challenges confronting teachers. Know the struggles. Feel the struggles. Be present. It is the only way to provide effective and meaningful support.

69

Behind every successful principal is a faculty and staff who are crushing it.

70

Leaders don't think of everything. They can't think of everything. They need to lean on their people . . . and they need to learn from their people.

71

It's hard to lead people who don't trust you. So, if you want to lead . . . build some relationships . . . and earn the trust.

72

Some would say administrators should visit classrooms because that is how they can provide "instructional leadership." That may be true. But I think they should visit classrooms, if for no other reason, so they always remember how challenging the work of teaching is.

73

When someone is talking to you, the subject might not rank high on your priority list. But to them, it can be their whole world. Good leaders are able to recognize, appreciate, and validate the questions and challenges of everyone in the organization.

74

Teachers don't know our values by what we say. They know our values by what we do.

75

Leaders . . . there can be a fine line between challenging teachers to "push the envelope of excellence" and causing them to feel inadequate. We need to be aware of that tension. Our goal is inspiring teachers . . . but when we're not in touch with our staff, we can overwhelm them.

76

We talk about the importance of teachers developing relationships with students. But it's also important for administrators to develop relationships with their teachers. That is how they support them . . . how they encourage them . . . how they lead them. It is how culture is built.

77

It's not easy being an effective teacher. Good administrators spend time walking their school and hanging out in classrooms . . . and they pick up on that fact quickly.

78

Leadership is not always about having all the answers . . . or articulating bold visions. Sometimes it's just about providing relentless support to those in the trenches.

79

Complex problems do not usually have simple answers. Good leaders recognize that "quick fixes" are not the goal . . . and they understand that meaningful solutions are usually the result of collaborating with others in the organization, thoughtfully analyzing the issues.

80

Our teachers inspire me. If you're an administrator, and your teachers don't inspire you . . . you need to get into classes more . . . 'cause they're working really hard.

81

What are the conditions in which teachers thrive? This is the question that should drive school leaders. The most effective administrators put their blood, sweat, and tears into creating this type of environment. And then their teachers are empowered to do the same for the kids.

82

Leaders . . . if you want to change the behavior of those you lead, perhaps you should try changing the way you lead them. If you're a leader, it starts with you.

83

Good leadership is not necessarily about figuring out how to improve those around you; it's about creating the conditions where those around you can improve themselves.

84

If you want to be an effective leader, you need to be excited about the journey . . . not just the destination.

85

Every leader is flawed. I think they are actually more effective when they can acknowledge that. It's a bit ironic . . . but vulnerability can be a sign of strength.

86

People may hear your words, and they may read your words. But that doesn't mean they know your heart. What really matters is what you do and how you treat others. It's the example you set. The life you lead is always more powerful than the speech you give.

87

Before they buy into your vision, they have to first buy into you. Whether it's a teacher in a classroom, a coach on a ball field, or a principal in a faculty meeting . . . good leaders never shortchange the process of establishing credibility and building rapport.

88

I'm not always sure what "instructional leadership" looks like . . . and I'm not always certain about what teachers expect from the instructional leader. But I am always certain that they want me to care about them, their students, and the challenges they face in the classroom.

89

I don't think there are many people who wake up with a goal of doing a poor job at work. Most people are doing the best job they know how. It is the leader's job to accept staff for who they are at the moment . . . and give them the tools, resources, training, and encouragement they need to grow.

90

It takes a lot of time to develop engaging lessons. It takes a lot of energy to stay upbeat for all the students. It takes a lot of patience to handle some of the knuckleheads. I hope there is no principal out there who takes their teachers for granted.

91

When administrators spend time in classrooms, they are reminded how much those teachers have to plan, how much they have to manage, and how unbelievably patient they are. Teachers are the heart and soul of every school.

92

We don't always have it together as leaders. Sometimes we're just fumbling our way through . . . trying to do right by those around us.

93

Good leaders are not preoccupied with their position . . . they're preoccupied with their people.

94

Good principals are not so much about making their teachers better. They are about unlocking the passion and creativity that teachers already have.

95

Good principals bring out the best in their teachers. Those teachers are not driven to comply; they're inspired to grow.

96

Never miss an opportunity to brag about your colleagues to the visitors in the building. And preferably . . . do it in front of the colleagues.

97

Principals should spend far more energy catching their teachers doing the right thing than doing the wrong thing.

98

The most important thing for principals to understand is that the teachers are the most important resource in the building.

99

I think it's probably a good thing for educators to reevaluate which school rules and classroom rules are really worth having.

100

There is not a way to improve the culture without improving the relationships. The latter always drives the former.

101

I love the fact that every day we go to work, we can make a difference. Maybe not a big difference. But lots of little differences. And those add up. We can support a colleague, connect with a kid, make someone smile . . . or make their burden a little lighter. That can be tomorrow!

102

One of the definitions of a *professional* is "someone who gets after it even when they're not really feeling the passion." 'Cause there's gonna be days when we're not feelin' it . . . but we still gotta get after it.

103

We are not responsible for the attitude of those around us. But we do have the opportunity to affect the attitude of those around us.

104

We wake up . . . we go to work . . . we are kind to those around us . . . we come home and love our family. We make our little corner of the world a better place because we are here. That is what we do.

105

I think it's important to trust people to do their job. And I think it's important to assume people want to be good at their job. While that might not always be the case, I think any other assumption undermines a healthy culture. I could be wrong; it's just my philosophy.

106

If people don't know I love my job, I'm not doing it right.

107

Sometimes what our students need most is for us to encourage them and to support them . . . to instill in them the confidence that they can do it!

108

If you want to build your culture . . . invest in your people. It's not about the programs, plans, or even the strategies; it's always about the people.

109

Some days are good accidentally. But you can also have good days on purpose. Today could be one of those.

110

Your colleagues need to know that they are not alone. No one should struggle in isolation. And you can still build a positive culture in the face of adversity. This is the magic of camaraderie. It is the beauty of knowing that we're all doing this together. And we're not alone.

111

The first step in effective leadership is finding your passion for the vision. People follow passion . . . not plans.

112

The best principals understand that their job has no inherent value. Their job is valuable only inasmuch as they help teachers do their job better.

113

When your values align with your actions . . . you are authentic. It's that simple.

114

The best leaders don't solve all the problems . . . but they engage others in a collective pursuit of solutions.

115

Teachers know what their principal values by observing how the principal spends time.

116

If you work in a school, you are important to more than just the kids. Staff morale is not usually a function of the students . . . but of the level of support, encouragement, trust, respect, and camaraderie that exists among the adults in the building.

117

When I look at people who are successful in their profession, they seem to really enjoy their work. Rather than trudging along, going through the motions . . . their work actually energizes them.

118

Sometimes the most passionate educators are the ones most grateful for encouragement. They invest themselves so totally in their students that they get sucked dry. Being reminded about the value of their work can lift the spirit of a weary teacher.

119

Appropriate thinking comes before appropriate acting. I think it's a mistake to focus on behavior without first understanding the values that drive the behavior. And I think this dynamic applies to kids and adults alike.

120

Something I love about strong school culture: it builds capacity . . . capacity to adapt and to grow. We don't know what the future holds, and we can't always predict what our students will need. But the right school culture will make it possible for us to rise to the challenge.

121

Don't underestimate the value of camaraderie. And don't wait for someone to be a great colleague to you. It's always a good day to be a great colleague to someone else.

122

When someone around you screws up, and they already feel bad about it . . . it's usually not constructive to kick them when they're down. Sometimes grace is more transformative than justice.

123

Leadership is about creating a sense of urgency to rise above the status quo . . . and empowering others to join you in the journey.

124

Teachers buy into the principal before they buy into the principal's vision. Don't underestimate the relationships. Don't underestimate the process.

125

School administrators can't build culture by themselves . . . but they can certainly set the right tone. And that tone is:

- Admin supports the teachers.
- The teachers collaborate to support the students.
- We're gonna have fun doing it.

126

In good schools, the teachers and the administration are invested in each other's success. They respect each other, and they appreciate each other . . . because they realize that they're all in it for the same reason: the KIDS!

127

I believe that the single best way to transform a school is to cultivate collaboration between the adults in the building. When the teachers are working together for the good of the kids . . . they can make magic.

128

~~~~~

Every school has the same mission: preparing kids for their future . . . What matters is not the quality of words in the frame but the quality of relationships in the building.

129

~~~~~

Something will go wrong for you today . . . which means you will have the opportunity to demonstrate resilience to those around you. So that's a cool thing.

130

You can transform your school's culture for free. It doesn't cost anything to focus on the kids. It doesn't cost anything to collaborate. And it doesn't cost anything to keep a positive attitude.

131

Students want support from teachers. Teachers want support from administrators. Administrators want support from central office. If you're ever in that situation, and you don't know what to do . . . it's hard to go wrong if you offer support.

132

When you encourage your students, you are building culture. When you encourage your colleagues, you are building culture. A little bit of encouragement goes a long way in creating schools where kids enjoy learning and adults enjoy working.

133

We can't control our supervisors, our funding, or our parents. We do control our enthusiasm and our commitment. Our students need us to focus on what we control.

134

It's good when administrators assume that teachers want to be excellent in their job. It's good when teachers assume that their students want to succeed in school. High expectations usually help others become the best version of themselves.

135

Encouragement is the greatest form of motivation. Never underestimate the power of your words.

136

When you stop thinking about your own problems and focus on how you can improve the lives of others, you make your own life more meaningful.

137

It's good to have high expectations of others. It's imperative that we have high expectations of ourselves.

138

There's a difference between writing a good lesson plan and being a good teacher. And there's a difference between writing a good school improvement plan and being a good leader. The difference is found in the human connections.

139

It's important to have long-range plans. But it is probably more important to be nice to the person in front of you.

140

I hope to encourage others to think about things that matter; remind others to focus on what they can control; and inspire others to continue making a difference.

141

When teachers are sick or if they have a sick child, they should not feel guilty about staying home. The school will go on without them. It's important that we encourage teachers to take care of their own families.

142

It doesn't matter what program you have in your school. The success of that program is a result of the adult leading it. Adults are always the variable.

143

If you want to create a good school culture, do these three things:

1 Always make decisions based on what's good for the students.
2 Always foster collaboration between the adults in the building.
3 Always bring positive energy to work.

144

The value of a teacher cannot be reduced to the quality of their lesson . . . and a student certainly cannot be reduced to the quality of their test score.

145

Teachers are more motivated when their administration supports them, values them, and encourages them. Guess when students are more motivated.

146

I think the most powerful instructional leadership can be seen in the collaboration of teachers who are motivating each other to raise the bar. Positive peer pressure from colleagues is more meaningful than supervisory pressure from administrators.

147

There are no perfect educators . . . but when my teachers are looking out for kids . . . when they're trying to improve their instruction . . . when they are staying positive . . . they are perfect to me.

148

I recommend giving yourself opportunities to be inspired. You do this by figuring out ways to hang around passionate educators who share your values.

149

Many students feel overwhelmed. Their teachers should understand how that feels . . . because many of them feel overwhelmed as well. And yep . . . any administrator who recognizes his or her challenges feels overwhelmed too. We should all just be patient with each other.

150

The synergy that results between passionate teachers and supportive administrators is ridiculously awesome. It is what drives great schools.

151

Sometimes bad stuff happens to me . . . and sometimes I get discouraged. But I don't choose to focus on that stuff. I don't think it's constructive. My hope is to stay focused on why I do what I do . . . and how I can encourage others to remember their "why" as well.

152

Teachers and administrators do not become exceptional by accident. They work hard at their job. They reflect on their work and are constantly learning. They collaborate with colleagues to make stronger decisions. And they cultivate meaningful relationships with their students.

153

When you're looking for compliance . . . you'll never find excellence.

154

There's a good chance that someone will call in sick tomorrow . . . who doesn't have a sub. We can complain about it . . . or we can pick up the slack and get busy making the most of the time we have.

155

Maintaining a positive attitude at work does not mean you're in denial about how bleak the reality of the situation may be. It means you're choosing to focus on your potential for making a difference rather than dwelling on the negative circumstances that you can't control.

156

Don't worry about the curriculum, the instruction, or the assessments . . . if you don't have a good culture. You can focus on that stuff if you want . . . but you'll be barking up the wrong tree. The right culture allows the other stuff to even BE possible.

157

We want to be educators with no regrets. We don't want to regret not making that phone call home . . . or not going to that game . . . or not saying, "I'm so proud of you," . . . or not asking, "Are you really OK?" We don't want to leave the acts undone . . . or the words unsaid.

158

If you're a leader, I think it's important you create a culture where people feel free to tell you what you NEED to hear . . . not necessarily what you WANT to hear.

159

You're a source of inspiration for some of your colleagues. I'm not sure which ones, though . . . and neither are you. I guess you should just assume all of them will benefit from your encouragement.

160

Administrators build relationships with their teachers the same way teachers do with their students. They talk to them; they invest time in them; they respect them; they value them; they support them. It doesn't have to be complicated . . . but it needs to be a priority.

161

It's good when central office admins remember what it's like to work in a school. It's good when school admins remember what it's like to be a teacher. It's good when teachers remember what it's like to be a student. The students . . . they're just trying to get through their day.

162

Maintaining a positive attitude doesn't necessarily solve the problems . . . but it usually puts you in a better frame of mind to find solutions . . . and it makes you a lot more fun to be around.

163

School culture is something that we control. That's what I love about it. We all can contribute to a stronger school culture simply by being intentional with what we value and with how we spend our time.

164

Today, we won't be able to control the weather, the attitudes of the kids, or the number of annoying emails that flood our inbox. But . . . we can control the number of times we smile, the number of high fives we give, and the energy we bring to work. We actually control a lot!

165

If you can go through the day taking steps to ensure that those around you feel valued . . . you will have had a meaningful day. Sleep well.

166

We think we accept others; we think we embrace others; we think we love others. But it doesn't really matter if they don't feel it. Our good intentions are not enough . . . 'cause it's not about us.

167

We may not know the story of those we meet. We may not know all their joys or all their struggles. Recognizing this truth is the first step toward empathy. It is an important step toward elevating their humanity. It is the recognition that they do have a story . . . and it has value.

168

Good leaders don't lead from their office. They lead in the hallway . . . in the classrooms . . . in the cafeteria . . . and in the bus line. Good leaders are present and always engaged.

169

When people are excited about what they do, when they are mindful of why they do it, and when they genuinely care about those they are with . . . cool stuff happens.

170

There are some things in your life that you may end up regretting. But investing yourself in other people will probably not be one of them.

171

Educators talk a lot about the importance of building "relationships." What that really means is . . . we need to focus on PEOPLE. There's nothing magical about it . . . and there's certainly not a formula. Just value the people around you . . . and care about their wellbeing.

172

Being inspired is important. It fuels your passion and maximizes your impact. It generates the energy that those around you find compelling. So . . . figure out what inspires you . . . and run with it.

173

Nostalgia for the good ole days is not constructive. We have awesome kids today! They need our best today! So we can give them a better tomorrow.

174

When we take time to build relationships with the adults around us, it doesn't really have anything to do with student achievement. But it has everything to do with culture. And in the right culture, teachers will thrive, students will thrive . . . and the achievement will increase.

175

Sometimes . . . kids are just trying to make it through their day. Teachers need to understand this. And sometimes . . . teachers are just trying to make it through their day. Administrators need to understand this.

176

School culture is not a function of the resources in the building; it is a function of the attitudes in the building.

177

For me, remaining "positive" is not about always having a great day or a perfect attitude. (We all have rough days.) But it is about keeping things in perspective. And it is about an abiding certainty that we can choose to make a difference every day in spite of the adversity.

178

One of my definitions of school culture goes like this: administrators give teachers the benefit of the doubt . . . and teachers give administrators the benefit of the doubt.

179

I think these are the types of things leaders should wonder about on their staff's behalf:

- I wonder how I could support them more effectively.
- I wonder what I could do to make their job easier.
- I wonder how I could inspire them to reach for awesome.
- I wonder what they wish I understood about them.

180

We all prefer to be around those people who make us feel better about ourselves. I hope our students feel better about themselves because they were in our class . . . because they were in our school.

181

When you put yourself out there . . . you may fail. You may be ridiculed. You may fall flat on your face. But excellence is not achieved by those who play it safe all the time. So here's to those who are willing to risk it . . . to those who choose courage and accept vulnerability.

182

We all have a limited perspective. We see things through the lens of our own experiences and with our own biases. It's important to be mindful of this reality and engage others with a sense of humility. Give folks the same benefit of the doubt that you would like from them.

183

School culture is nothing more than the values of the adults in the building . . . put into action. How do you put your values into action?

184

Someone once asked me, "How do you stay so positive?" Well . . . I have hard days like everyone else; that's the reality. But I still love students and teachers; that's also the reality. We don't get to choose our circumstances. But we always get to choose what we focus on.

185

When I walk into a school, and it becomes obvious to me that the adults enjoy working there, I immediately suspect it's a good place for students. Strong staff morale reflects a strong culture . . . and that's an environment that is good for kids . . . and for their learning.

186

Sometimes there are circumstances in your work environment that are awful. That's the reality. Most of those circumstances are out of your control. That's also the reality. Keep caring about students. Keep supporting your colleagues. Don't overlook the little moments of joy.

187

Keep your head in the game. This week, you may find yourself distracted by drama in the school. You may find yourself frustrated with a colleague or aggravated with a student. If this is the case, try to remember how important your job is . . . and keep your head in the game.

188

Time invested in people will always be time well spent.

189

If you ask a teacher what they want from their admin, they're probably not gonna say, "Instructional leadership." Most will simply say, "SUPPORT!" It's important to note, though . . . that when they do feel supported, they are much more receptive to the instructional leadership.

190

When you make a mistake . . . fess up to it. It doesn't make you weak; it makes you strong.

191

Every time you make the person in front of you feel important . . . you're contributing to a stronger school culture.

192

You don't always have to teach . . . or lead . . . or inspire. Sometimes it's enough to listen . . . and care . . . and love.

193

Kids need to learn to be responsible, to be on time, to follow rules, etc. I get it. But please don't allow yourself to be consumed with tardies and dress code. These things will always be with you, and there are more meaningful things in the school that deserve your energy.

194

There are about 95 essential things you need to know in life. One of them is to be kind. The others you can figure out as you go.

195

You will encounter someone today who is having a hard day. But your interaction with them might make their load a little lighter. The conversations matter.

196

I think a great thing to do is ask the students in the school what they think the adults in the school need to know about them. Listening to what students have to say . . . and valuing what they have to say . . . goes a long way toward building a great school culture.

197

When we choose to be around passionate educators, good stuff happens. We are reminded that we're on the right track and we're not alone. We are inspired by new possibilities and motivated to elevate our game. And we provide encouragement to those around us to continue the journey.

198

You have some colleagues who are barely hanging on. They're just trying to keep their head above water. But you may not know which ones . . . so I recommend being gracious with all of them. And your students too.

199

Every time you interact with a student or colleague, you have an opportunity to make them feel special. That's some powerful potential that we all have.

200

These are the things I hope the kids are able to say about me:

"He was nice to us."
"He seemed to enjoy working here."
"He didn't mind being silly."
"He had high expectations for us."
"He went to bat for me when I needed help."
"He treated us all the same . . . with respect."

201

Sometimes our students are immature. Sometimes I'm immature too. We can be quick to judge kids when they're having a bad day. I suspect that we hold out hope that others are not so quick to judge us on our bad days.

202

Principals don't lead schools; they lead teachers. Just like teachers don't teach classes; they teach students. We're usually more effective when we are mindful of the distinction.

203

It doesn't really matter what staff are saying about us. In the end, the only thing we can control . . . is what we're saying about them. And what we're saying about them, should always be constructive. A legacy of building others up, always trumps a legacy of tearing others down.

204

We don't know what a week will bring . . . but we know what WE will bring! We will bring our energy, our patience, our sense of humor, and our passion. We will bring the AWESOME! We will teach . . . we will lead . . . and we will make a difference for the students!

205

I'm inspired by teachers who define their success by the success of their students . . . and express genuine care for kids. I'm inspired by administrators who bend over backward to support their teachers . . . and who have courage to rock the boat when needed.

206

Accountability is important. But so is grace. We all like it when others give us a break.

207

Think about what gives you hope . . . about what encourages you to think that tomorrow can be better than today . . . about what makes you feel like you're headed in the right direction and destined for something important. Now think about what gives your students that hope.

208

It's important that administrators practice the same flexibility and patience with teachers . . . that they expect those teachers to demonstrate to their students.

209

Awesomeness is in direct proportion to passion. You show me an educator who is passionate . . . and I'll show you an educator who brings the awesome.

210

Five ways to build culture:

1) Focus on finding solutions rather than complaining about problems.
2) Collaborate with others in decision-making.
3) Give colleagues the benefit of the doubt.
4) Celebrate little victories.
5) Always keep the focus on students.

211

I don't always have the right words . . . or the right answer . . . or the right strategy . . . but I hope to always have the right heart; a heart for students and a heart for teachers.

212

Every day you have opportunities to lift others up. Don't let them slip by. There will surely be days you need others to lift you up.

213

Reflecting on your year can be a good thing if it inspires joy and gratitude. If you had a hard year . . . let it go. You're moving on down the road.

214

When I'm having a hard day, I need to remember that those around me may be having hard days too. Maybe I can make their load a little lighter. And maybe when I focus on improving their day . . . my own day gets a little better.

215

What do you truly care about in your job? What is it that lights your fire? These are questions worth thinking about on a regular basis. They help us focus our time and energy on the things that matter most.

216

Most students probably couldn't tell you what school culture is. But they feel it . . . just like the adults.

217

Some insights should seem obvious, but they aren't. Some practices should come naturally, but they don't. Some changes should be easy, but they're not. We're all at different places . . . but we all learn, and we all grow.

218

It's easy to get preoccupied with what would, could, or should happen . . . next week, next month, or next year. But the present is where it's at! Right now is when we have the opportunity to make a difference.

219

I think it's important to be transparent with our values. Those around us need to know what we're about . . . what we believe in . . . and what we're committed to.

220

I believe all kids want to be successful. I believe teachers who view themselves as the most important variable in the classroom, have the biggest impact. I believe teachers are stronger when they collaborate. I believe administrators should support and reinforce the process.

221

I have learned that smiling at students and calling them by name goes a long way. This is not a profound truth . . . but it is an important one. Connecting with kids is a big deal. It doesn't take much . . . but it almost always starts with a smile.

222

Sometimes we feel like we are thriving. And sometimes we feel like we are just trying to keep out head above water. But whatever the day . . . we will interact with students and colleagues . . . which means we WILL make a difference. Every day counts!

223

I like laughing with teachers. I actually think it's important for administrators to laugh with their teachers from time to time . . . just as it is important for teachers to laugh with their students. You build culture with the little things . . . like laughter.

224

We have families, and we need to take care of them. We have personal lives outside of school that sustain us and bring us joy. Teachers should never feel guilty about investing time in their own kids. They should never feel guilty about spending time with those they care about.

225

When you focus on being good to the people you work with . . . there's a decent chance you will end up being great at your job. They may remember your ideas; they may remember your skill; they will always remember how you treated the people with whom you worked.

226

We talk about the value of "high fives" for kids. But I'm reminded that staff members need high fives too! We ALL benefit from encouragement . . . and we ALL want to feel connected.

227

"Thank you." This is such an important sentence. Only two words . . . but when they are spoken in sincerity, they say a lot. It's important to acknowledge the efforts of others . . . even when those efforts are in their "job description." We can't take our colleagues for granted.

228

The example you set encourages your colleagues to elevate their game. Or it doesn't. But make no mistake about it . . . your colleagues notice your game.

229

I think great administrators try to view things through the eyes of teachers . . . and I think great teachers try to view things through the eyes of students.

230

Some kids are gonna need extra help with their work this year . . . just like some teachers are gonna need extra help figuring out how to change their computer login. We all appreciate the patience of those around us. And sometimes . . . we all need others to cut us some slack.

231

You probably have students who aren't sure who they will be living with this year. You can't fix that . . . but it's good to know that reality. You probably have colleagues who have anxieties they aren't verbalizing. You can't fix that . . . but it's good to know that reality.

232

I don't think you can mandate excellence. So it seems to me that the goal is to create the conditions where folks want to choose excellence. And support them and encourage them along the way.

233

Patience . . . flexibility . . . support . . . and grace. If this is not what we're bringing to the table right now, then we're bringing the wrong stuff.

234

I hope educators feel free to invest in their family. Their own kids are still the most important students in their lives. And that's how it should be.

235

There are adults in your school today who are feeling awesome. And you also have colleagues who are barely hanging on. You might know the difference between them, and you might not. Educators can put on a good face. If you're struggling today . . . keep hangin' on. You've got this!

236

If you're alert, you'll discover that there are opportunities to be awesome all around you . . . opportunities to make someone's day. Building strong school culture is nothing more than making the most of all those small moments.

237

We all have flaws . . . but we all have a little bit of awesome. Be patient with the flaws of others . . . and celebrate their AWESOME.

238

The best thing teachers can do for their colleagues . . . is to bring a positive attitude to work every day. Positive energy is contagious.

239

Relationships are not generated out of thin air; they are cultivated through conversations . . . and are made stronger through vulnerability.

240

It's not enough to think that your team members are valuable. It's important to tell them. People need to know their work is appreciated.

241

As it turns out, the type of culture that creates the best learning environments for kids is also the best to recruit and retain great teachers.

242

I recommend dealing with difficult people the same way you deal with your favorites . . . with kindness, patience, respect, and understanding.

243

There are 57 reasons that school culture is important, but you only have to know one of them: it matters for kids.

244

Strategic plans don't improve schools; the passionate educators who carry them out do! People are always more valuable than plans.

245

Good school culture is never a fluke. It results from educators who love their job and make decisions based on the best interests of kids!

246

When principals are excited about leading, teachers are more likely to be excited about teaching, and students are more likely to be excited about learning.

247

You can probably do it alone, but you can probably do it better with someone else.

248

Good school culture is what results when the adults in the building are always mindful of why they come to work.

249

First, we figure out what's best for kids. Then, we figure out how to make it happen.

250

Good teachers are gracious with their students. Good principals are gracious with their teachers. The world is a better place when we are all gracious with one another.

251

When dealing with people, don't jump to conclusions. There's always more than meets the eye. Everyone has a story to tell.

252

We can't control the parents, the mandates, or the class size. We CAN control our instruction and the passion we bring for the kids.

253

Principals shape school culture . . . as do custodians, secretaries, counselors, teachers, bookkeepers, students, librarians, paraprofessionals, maintenance technicians, SROs, nurses, registrars, etc.

254

It would be cool if schools could figure out ways to validate curiosity more than they validate compliance.

255

Our educational practices should not be grounded in tradition; they should be grounded in what the research says is best for students. This is the difference between a job and a profession.

256

I'm grateful for teachers who are willing to re-evaluate their philosophy and practice in order to serve students more effectively and more appropriately. This is what professionals do . . . but I don't take it for granted.

257

Think about why you got into education. That purpose still holds up! Your reason for going to work each day is just as valuable now as it ever was. The mission hasn't changed . . . and it always matters.

258

One of the most important things we can do as humans . . . is to be curious about the perspective and experiences of other humans.

259

Some students aren't putting forth much effort; I'm grateful that teachers aren't giving up on them. Some parents keep pushing back; I'm grateful that teachers are demonstrating poise and patience. This year is really hard; I'm grateful that teachers are persevering.

260

Sometimes we take a position on something . . . but we really haven't considered all the angles. When we learn about the other angles . . . we need to be willing to change our position. Always look for the other angles.

261

We ask our students to be lifelong learners. Well . . . as educators are confronted with the reality of adapting to radically different instructional models . . . this is the perfect opportunity for us to practice what we preach and model for our students a little bit of "lifelong learning."

262

If we care about being educated, we need to take some personal responsibility for educating ourselves. I recommend reading and listening. And it's healthy to have our perspective challenged.

263

Crazy times like these are a testament to the importance of being resilient. It's good to remind students that their commitment to push through and push on . . . will be more important to their future than "intelligence" or "talent." You can share hope.

264

If you're kind, honest, and a hard worker . . . you'll end up being a great human. The academic standards are important . . . but it's also cool when educators can find ways to reinforce this other stuff.

265

We need to find more ways to recognize students for being dependable, for working hard, and for being kind. Those qualities will take them further in life than being on the honor roll.

266

A vision is only effective if it is shared. So it's not about the leader; it's about the team. It's about the values that are held in common. It's about the relationships that are built. And it's about the shared aspirations among everyone in the organization.

267

We want students to become lifelong learners. Well . . . it starts with us. The adults in the school should set the example of what it means to adapt, change, grow, and continue learning.

268

I appreciate people who are willing to change their mind. It reflects intellectual humility, courage, and honesty. It reflects a willingness to consider new evidence, new ideas, and new ways of thinking. We need more of that.

269

How do you keep quality instruction in the classrooms? By keeping quality teachers in the school. How do you keep quality teachers in the schools? By providing them with quality support and adequate compensation.

270

Most parents are doing the best job they know how. Most parents love their kids, care about their education, and want them to have the best possible future. Sometimes we just need to remind ourselves of that.

271

Don't just listen to people who make you feel good or make you feel comfortable. Listen to people who challenge you. They can make you better.

272

Some parents judge schools by the test scores. But there are a lot of parents who judge schools by the attitude of their child when they get home in the afternoon. We need to be working to raise student achievement . . . but we also need to be creating good experiences for kids.

273

It has been said that knowledge is power. But in the age of Google, knowledge can be cheap. What is powerful . . . is the ability to create it, evaluate it, apply it, and collaborate with others to capitalize on it.

274

It's good to have hope . . . and it's good to have dreams. But success doesn't come from hope and dreams; it comes from putting in the work. To be sure, the former gives us the passion and the energy to keep pushing . . . but it's never easy. Never underestimate the value of hard work.

275

Do what you're passionate about. If that doesn't make you money, then you'll also have to find a job because the bills will keep coming. But no matter what . . . figure out a way to pursue what fires you up.

276

Resiliency might be more important than talent. People who can bounce back from adversity have a huge advantage in life.

277

Someone took a chance on me and hired me as a teacher . . . and then as an assistant principal . . . and then as a principal. I am grateful. We all have benefited from those who took a chance on us . . . who believed in us!

278

It's easier to throw stones than it is to make tough decisions. And sometimes, being a leader involves coming to terms with the fact that any decision you make will be the "wrong" one to a whole lot of people.

279

When my career is over . . . I don't think I'll remember our test scores or our curriculum maps. But I WILL remember some kids, and some teachers . . . and custodians, and nurses, and secretaries, and paras, and counselors, and SROs, and CNP workers. It is the people that matters to me.

280

Building relationships with your students and staff is not that complicated. Talk to them. Care about them. Be genuine.

281

The concept of education is simple. We meet students where THEY are . . . and prepare them for THEIR future.

282

Education offers students a better life, and we can never lose sight of this ultimate purpose. It's not about grades, academic proficiency, or scores on a standardized test. We're here to provide students with a brighter future.

283

The only way I know to address burnout in teachers is to support them and encourage them . . . to remind them of the incredible difference they make for kids. But there is no way of getting around the fact that the work is hard . . . and can be emotionally draining.

284

It's a good idea for teachers to contemplate what "essential skills" technology will render obsolete. We need to be preparing kids for their future, not our past. Nostalgia can be a barrier to a relevant education.

285

Educators would do well to focus more on process and less on outcomes. Learning is a journey . . . not a destination.

286

Good educators are not victims of unfair mandates, unruly kids, or unsupportive parents. They are change agents . . . and they rise above the adversity.

287

We often spend more time with the students than the parents do. Parents are trusting us with their kids. What an awesome responsibility!

288

Some kids who were bad students make great employees. It's just that schools sometimes ask kids to do stuff they see as totally irrelevant.

289

Excellence is not accidental . . . it is a choice. And we have a moral imperative to show up and be awesome for our kids every day.

290

We want our students prepared for the real world. Well in the real world . . . you don't fill in a lot of bubbles.

291

Sometimes I make mistakes. But I keep learning. I hope we are all communicating and modeling this concept for our kids.

292

Having a child on the honor roll doesn't make you a good parent. Instilling the right values in your child does.

293

The best education is not defined by content knowledge . . . but by skill acquisition.

294

The mark of a great school is not how much all the kids have learned . . . but how well the kids are prepared to keep learning.

295

The ultimate goal of education is not to teach kids everything they need to know . . . it's to prepare them to continue learning.

296

There is never a bad time to remember why we do what we do.

297

The strategies and practices of educators may change over time, but I suspect that the core values that inspire great teachers transcend the decades.

298

Education is not just about teaching the "curriculum." It's also about providing students with experiences that enrich their lives and expand their horizons.

299

Employers don't care about your GPA or your test scores. They care if you show up to work on time, follow directions, and work hard.

300

Education is no longer about teaching kids what they need to know. It is about letting them practice the things that they need to be able to do.

301

You don't always have to be awesome. Some days, it's an accomplishment just showing up.

302

I regret there may have been times over my career, where I corrected a student's language (so they could sound more middle class) . . . and it came across to them like I was devaluing them as a person . . . or their family . . . or their neighborhood. When we know better, we do better.

303

There are so many good kids in our schools! Sweet kids who make good choices. But it's easy for the adults in the building to get distracted, discouraged, or overwhelmed by the challenging ones. It's important to recognize and value the students doing the right things.

304

Students have told me repeatedly that they want their teachers and administrators to be involved. It's quite simple, really. We like for them to be engaged, and they like for us to be engaged.

305

Sometimes kids push their boundaries. That's what they do. Most adults were kids once. It's good to remember.

306

Students appreciate it when adults talk to them as if they were normal people.

307

I hope every student in our school feels like they have a voice. I hope every student feels like they have something to contribute. I hope every student feels like they matter. This is our job. It is my job. We need to create this type of school.

308

Teachers care about their students, and they understand that connecting with students is more important than ever. But they cannot carry the weight of the responsibility for the social and emotional health of all their kids. That's too much to bear. It takes a village.

309

There are some kids I can't figure out how to motivate. I just can't seem to get through to them. Maybe you have some of those students too. I don't know the answer . . . but I do know this: we must keep supporting them; we must keep encouraging them; and we must keep loving them.

310

Sometimes what students need most is a cheerleader . . . someone they know is in their corner. Sometimes that's what teachers need too.

311

I think the best way to inspire teachers is to remind them of their purpose. KIDS. I will never get tired of talking about the teachers' potential to make a difference for kids. They are our REASON. They are our true motivation. We can't ever forget that.

312

We have great kids in our school. And you have great kids in your school. I think it's important for educators to be optimistic about their students . . . to have high expectations for their students . . . and to believe in their future.

313

Teaching is challenging. It is stressful. It is exhausting. It is draining. The struggle of teachers is real. But so is their impact.

314

Sometimes teachers don't bring their "A-game" because of drama at their own home. I wonder why our kids don't always have their "A-game."

315

There are some things in my job that I regret. But taking time to connect with students is not one of them.

316

Fridays are great for teachers. But for some kids, school is a safer place than home. They're ready for Monday. We can't forget that.

317

Some things are more important than academics . . . like the physical and emotional well-being of a student. We all need to be sensitive to how kids are really feeling. Some of them are dealing with a lot.

318

I've learned a lot of things as a principal . . . but the big one is this: teachers are the most important resource in the school. They need to be supported, encouraged, and celebrated. They drive the school.

319

Think about the colleague who always encourages you . . . who always builds you up . . . who always makes you feel better about yourself. Then think about the unbelievable potential you have with each of your staff members.

320

I remember one of our teachers teaching a brilliant lesson. Everyone was engaged! And then a kid threw up. Just keepin' it real. The teacher responded with poise and care. Great teaching isn't always about an innovative lesson; sometimes it's about resilience and compassion.

321

We don't need our teachers to be the most talented, the most innovative, or the most tech savvy. We need them to care about kids . . . work well with their colleagues . . . and come to work every day, excited about making a difference.

322

I'm more convinced than ever . . . that a friendly smile and genuine greeting to the students we encounter during the day is more meaningful than most of us realize. It doesn't take much to inject some positivity into a kid's day.

323

Some kids don't seem motivated, and some kids have an attitude. Some adults give up on them, and some adults don't. The adults who persist are the ones who get to change lives.

324

Disrespect is never the core issue. It's always a symptom of something deeper. It's easy for the adults in the school to lose sight of that . . . but we can't.

325

Good teachers are also leaders. And good leaders are also teachers. They both need conviction, passion, and enthusiasm.

326

A student bombs a test. Teacher #1 responds, "What did you think was going to happen when you sleep in class and don't study?" Teacher #2 responds, "You can do so much better! I believe in you!" The way we interact with students matters. Our words matter. Are we reinforcing the low expectations that students have of themselves . . . or are we giving them hope?

327

"I'm so proud of you!" We should figure out ways to tell our students this as often as possible. It can have a significant impact on future behaviors and future attitudes. Plus . . . it can make a kid's day.

328

Teaching is not a job for those who don't love kids. Administration is not a job for those who don't love teachers. And you can't fake it.

329

I think leaders who obsess over loyalty are fundamentally insecure. I find that when leaders have integrity and make decisions based on the best interest of those they lead, they inspire loyalty.

330

Making decisions without collaborating is the biggest way to stunt organizational growth.

331

I think it's usually a bad idea for leaders to issue blanket admonitions to the entire staff when it's really about one offender. It usually makes the conscientious employees feel guilty, and the offender probably isn't listening.

332

"Please just let me teach!" School leaders need to recognize and appreciate this passionate plea that is felt by so many conscientious educators. And they should never stop exploring ways to minimize and streamline the extra paperwork.

333

Effective leaders are engaged without micromanaging. They are involved without being overbearing.

334

As administrators . . . most of us are just making it up as we go. There's not a manual for the stuff we deal with each day. We just try to support the teachers and do right by the kids. Just trying to employ empathy, love, and common sense.

335

I remember a conference with a parent about the handling of a discipline issue with their kid. After listening to the parent's points, I changed my mind. Frankly, the parent's points were stronger than my points. We don't always get it right the first time. Sometimes we need to change.

336

Administrators need to make sure their teachers feel supported. If they don't . . . not much else matters. I can assure you those teachers don't care about "instructional leadership."

337

When I drop by a classroom, I always try to spend more time watching the students than the teacher. Ultimately . . . that's all that matters . . . kids who are engaged and learning.

338

Great leaders create a sense of urgency to rise above the status quo. They inspire others to do more . . . to be more . . . to want more.

339

Great school leaders are usually characterized by these two things: 1) they support their teachers . . . always have their back and 2) they inspire their teachers . . . continuously reminding them of their core purpose . . . making a difference for kids.

340

Good leaders trust their people. Period. If they don't . . . they will end up micromanaging, and that sabotages morale.

341

I have never heard of someone at the end of their life wishing they had spent more time at work. We should love our job . . . but we should love our family more. I hope we never lose track of our priorities.

342

~~~~~~

Leaders don't always need enthusiasm . . . only when they want followers.

343

~~~~~~

I think principals should connect with kids . . . but they should also connect with teachers. Teachers need their support and encouragement too.

344

You can't be a great principal if you don't love teachers. They do the core business of the school, and it's crucial that they feel valued.

345

Authentic leaders don't have to talk about their core values. Everyone already knows leaders' core values based on their actions.

346

Good leaders are not remembered for their plans or their programs . . . they are remembered for their passion and their sense of purpose.

347

There is no substitute for authenticity. You have to genuinely care about the people in your organization.

348

Good leaders don't have all the answers . . . but they're committed to asking important questions.

349

If you have ever had someone send you an encouraging note . . . totally out of the blue . . . than you know what a cool thing it is. Never underestimate the value of encouraging words. That's all.

350

We all know that kids in the school have "reputations." Well . . . the adults have reputations too. I hope to be known as the one who always brings positive energy, the one who is a great team player, and the one who is all about the kids. How are you known in the halls of your school?

351

We need to be careful about passing judgment on others . . . their values, their decision-making, and their thought process . . . when we have not lived the lives they have lived. I think it's better to focus on connection, understanding, and relationship. That's when we move forward.

352

Good leaders pick up trash that they didn't put there. They lead by example. That's just what they do.

353

I hope that nobody is ever confused about what my values are . . . because I try to be transparent. And if you visit our school, I hope there is never any ambiguity about what we stand for. We are about the kids . . . making connections, building relationships, and changing lives.

354

～～～

It's good to have fun at work . . . practical jokes, inside jokes, corny jokes, music, shenanigans, hijinks, tomfoolery, silliness . . . and lots of laughing. Colleagues who have fun together, work hard together. And ultimately, it's a good culture in which students can learn.

355

～～～

The awareness that one's own experiences are not necessarily the experiences of others is an important one for educators to cultivate. It's important for other humans too.

356

Today, you'll have an opportunity to help a student or a colleague bounce back from a stressful night.

357

Much of our job is routine. Days come and go. There are moments, however, when I am keenly aware that I have the potential to change a kid's life. And here's the thing . . . as educators, we have more of these moments than we will ever know.

358

Some say focus on data-driven decisions. Some say focus on research-based instructional strategies. Some say focus on a 21st century curriculum. I say . . . focus on kids!

359

It's cool when we are able to give students opportunities to learn. It's cooler when we are able to give them opportunities to feel connected.

360

I love the fact that, no matter how bad our "to-do list" gets screwed up, no matter how many times the copier breaks, no matter how many times there's a spill in the hallway . . . we always have the ability to be nice to kids . . . to make them smile. I love that.

361

The little stuff matters. For teachers, thinking about how they will connect with students . . . this is important to remember. For administrators, trying to support their staff . . . this is important to remember.

362

Some days, I don't have the answer. Sometimes I'm not able to solve the problem. We have some tough challenges in our profession . . . but we don't give up. We must not give up. We'll get back after it tomorrow.

363

We all need to vent from time to time . . . including me. But I hope my venting never turns into a pattern of complaining. I hope I'm never responsible for bringing negative energy into the school. I hope I never wallow in self-pity. I hope I always keep things in perspective.

364

I regret those times that I passed a student in the hallway and didn't really acknowledge them. We should never be too busy or too distracted to acknowledge a kid.

365

Good leaders inspire others to support the vision. Great leaders empower others to own the vision.

Index of Quotes by Topic

Topic	Quote Numbers
School culture	6, 8, 9, 17, 18, 19, 28, 33, 58, 64, 65, 99, 100, 105, 107, 108, 110, 116, 120, 125, 127–128, 130, 132, 143, 156, 158, 163, 174, 176, 178, 183, 185, 191, 196, 210, 216, 223, 236, 241, 243, 245, 248, 253, 354
Supporting and appreciating your staff	2, 3, 4, 7, 12, 14, 16, 24, 31, 34, 38, 40–44, 46, 49, 51, 52, 54, 55–57, 61, 63, 66–69, 75–76, 78, 90, 91, 94–98, 115, 118, 121, 122, 124, 131, 134, 142, 141, 149, 150, 159,160, 168, 170, 171, 175, 179, 188, 189, 208, 220, 224, 225, 226, 227, 239, 240, 269, 283, 311, 313, 314, 318, 319, 320, 321, 332, 336, 339, 343, 344
Connecting with students	1, 5, 50, 180, 249, 263, 264–267, 290, 299, 300, 301–310, 312, 315, 316, 317, 322–324, 326, 327, 337, 357, 358, 359, 360, 364, 200–201, 221
Effective leadership	10, 11, 13, 15, 20–22, 23, 25–27, 29–30, 32, 35–37, 39, 45, 47–48, 53, 59, 60, 62, 70–74, 77, 79, 80–89, 92–93, 101–104, 106, 109, 111–114, 117, 119, 123, 126, 129, 133, 135, 136–140, 144–148, 151–155, 157, 161–162, 164–167, 169, 172–173, 177, 181–182, 184, 186–187, 190, 192–195, 197–199, 202–207, 209, 211–215, 217–219, 222, 228–235, 238, 242, 244, 246–247, 250–252, 253, 255–262, 268, 271, 273–282, 284–286, 288, 289, 291, 293–298, 325, 328–331, 333, 334, 340–342, 345–353, 355, 356, 361–363, 365
Understanding parents	270, 272, 287, 292, 335, 338

Printed in the United States
by Baker & Taylor Publisher Services